1849–1879

# Thirty Years Ago

George D. Dornin, from a daguerreotype by Kilbourne.
Nevada City, November, 1852.

1849–1879

# Thirty Years Ago

BY

GEORGE D. DORNIN

Gold Rush Memories of a Daguerreotype Artist

*Edited by Peter E. Palmquist*

CARL MAUTZ PUBLISHING
NEVADA CITY
1995

*First published in 1873*
*First softcover edition, 1995*



*Cover photograph: Nevada City, 1852, daguerreotype by George D. Dornin.*
*Collection of the California State Library*
*Back cover photograph: North San Juan, half-plate daguerreotype by George D. Dornin.*
*Collection of the Seales Historical Library, Nevada City, California.*

LIBRARY OF CONGRESS CATALOG CARD NUMBER: 95-78477

LIBRARY OF CONGRESS CATALOGING-IN-PUBLICATION DATA
Dornin, George D., 1830-1907
Thirty years ago: reminiscences of a Gold Rush daguerreotype artist / George Dornin. —Carl Mautz Pub., 1995.
p. cm.
Reprint of 1873 ed.
ISBN: 1-887694-00-5
1. Dornin, George D., 1830-1907. 2. California—History.
3. Photographers—Biography. I. Title.
F865.D67 1995 979.4'04
QBI95-20344

*Carl Mautz Publishing*
*229 Commercial Street, No. 522*
*Nevada City, California 95959*

*Telephone (916) 478-1610*
*Facsimile (916) 478-0466*
*E-Mail FolkImage@aol.com*

ACKNOWLEDGEMENT

*The publisher would like to thank Mr. Edwin L. Tyson and the Searles Historical Library for their kind cooperation in allowing the use of George D. Dornin's daguerreotype view of North San Juan.*

Reprinted in celebration of
the annual meeting of
The Daguerreian Society,
Oakland, California,
October 27-29, 1995

# PREFACE

*FEW autobiographical accounts of gold-rush California are as interesting and wonderfully detailed as George D. Dornin's* THIRTY YEARS AGO. *Born in New York City on December 30, 1830, Dornin spent his early years, beginning at age 13, as an office boy and clerk on Wall Street. He had barely passed his eighteenth birthday when he set out in January 1849 for adventure on the shores of what he hoped would be his personal "El Dorado" of opportunity and good fortune. Equipped with three pair of "stogy boots" in graduated sizes ("I was yet a 'growing' boy"), he also carried his mother's daguerreotype likeness, over which he wept "often and bitterly" during his lengthy passage around Cape Horn. ¶ When he arrived in San Francisco on August 8, 1849, he was penniless, yet disdained the beckoning gold fields for a variety of odd jobs in the city itself. In fact, Dornin's riveting accounts of his entrepreneurial activities form a significant and valuable portion of his overall narrative: launderer, sign painter, baker, wallpaper hanger, et al. He operated and sold a lunch stand, established a combined restaurant/outfitter store, only to lose everything to the great fire of May 4, 1851. Undaunted, he reverted to odd jobs before agreeing to work, without salary, toward a share in a jewelry store. He conducted a lottery of jewelry for the store in Nevada City in the summer of 1852 but ran afoul of a local anti-lottery law. While this latest setback succeeded in ruining his dream of returning east with his pockets full of gold by 1852, it induced him to settle permanently in California. ¶ Dornin became a merchant in Nevada City, next a daguerreotypist in Grass Valley and North San Juan. An active Republican, Dornin served four years in the state legislature, concurrently working as an express agent, telegraph operator, bookkeeper, and owner-operator of two local stage lines. His ultimate career, however, was as a highly successful insurance agent. He died in 1907 after a long and productive life in which he gave thanks "for the often advantages which have followed seeming disasters; and the silver lining which has often illumined the darker clouds of my life . . ."*

PETER E. PALMQUIST
Arcata, California, April, 1995

Geo. D. Dornin

1849–1879

# Thirty Years Ago

THESE REMINISCENCES of "Early Days in California" are written up for my children, for whom, perhaps, they may have especial interest in the after years, when the days of the Argonauts, and the events attending the settlement of California, will appear as a chapter of romance. Outside of my own family circle, they have no particular value, nor are they intended to present any claim to literary excellence; they are simply an effort to put on record, so far as memory will serve, the events which led a young man to undertake the long journey to far-away California; the impressions which the new City of San Francisco (then just emerging from its chrysalis state as Yerba Buena) left upon him; and, the vicissitudes of Pioneer life which he encountered.

A faithfully kept "Log-Book" would prove a valuable adjunct at this time, but that, with many cherished letters and memoranda, was destroyed in the great fire in Grass Valley, which burned my dwelling in 1855; hence, the memory, not very tenacious, can alone be made available.

The first reports concerning the discovery of Gold, which I can remember, reached me in October or November, 1848.

I was then a lad, approaching my eighteenth year, having been born in the City of New York on the 30th day of December, 1830.

For nearly five years previous to the first mentioned period, I had been an office boy or clerk in various offices or business houses in Wall and William Streets—for the longest period in the employ of Jos. Dupre & Co., Importers of French Goods.

While in this establishment, and during the summer of 1848, I was much in the company of Mr. J. W. Tucker, a gentleman some seven or eight years my senior, who, at that time, sold fine cutlery, pocket-books, etc., on the steps of the National Bank in Wall Street, to which Bank, my uncle, William H. Dornin, had been for many years attached.

I occasionally met Mr. Tucker also at my uncle's residence in Bloomingdale. This gentleman had the true Connecticut Yankee's enterprise, and among his many projects was a trip to Texas, in which I was promised a part; my boyish love for change and taste for adventure being greatly increased thereby. As I now look back at those days, I am led to believe that there was no substantial basis for the promised journey to Texas, but it served the purpose of rendering me restless and dissatisfied with the slow, humdrum life about me, so that when the first faint rumors began to circulate, that far-away on the western edge of the continent, Gold without limit could be had for the digging, I was ripe and ready to go, if the means could be had to provide for the journey.

The rumors of the gold discoveries received confirmation in the official report of the Acting and Military Governor, General Mason, to the Secretary of War, and the Gold Fever immediately became epidemic.

"Ho, for California!" was the rallying cry throughout the civilized world, inviting the enterprising, the adventurer, whatever might be his condition; the uprising was as if by magic; wherever, and as rapidly as, the news spread, men turned and joined the Great Migration toward the Golden State. Not since the days of the Crusades has such an uprising taken place, and like the Crusaders, the pilgrims were (with rare exceptions) men—young men, or under the middle age.

In New York, as in other sea-board cities, ships were immediately fitted up for transportation of passengers around Cape Horn; large numbers, and those mainly of the interior States, chose the equally long and quite as hazardous journey across the plains, or through Mexico, while the route, via the Isthmus of Panama, was so thronged with emigrants as to preclude the possibility of finding connecting vessels at the

Pacific ports.

The newspapers were crowded with advertisements of California Outfits, California Hats and California Pistols. Companies for mining and trading were formed, with elaborate laws and rules, and equipped with tents, provisions, and machinery for extracting the gold; these, I may here say, by way of parenthesis, were generally disbanded on or before their arrival in California, and the gold-washing machinery, which was rarely of practical use, was strewn along the beach in San Francisco Bay.

Many persons were fitted out, by more prosperous friends at home, or agreements to share all gains for periods of greater or less duration; no terms, in the eagerness of all parties, seeming too extravagant.

My impatience to be off grew as winter approached, every day's delay seeming precious time wasted. Of the several routes, that by way of Cape Horn was finally settled upon, and through the kind offices of my uncle, the means were advanced to pay for my passage and outfit.

A Mr. John H. Turney, connected with the City Bank of New York, was expected to form one of the party, but he selected the route via Mexico, it being understood that we were to meet and remain together in California.

These preliminaries were arranged in December, 1848, and in January, 1849, my passage was secured by the payment of $135 to the Association which had purchased and fitted out the good ship *Panama*, commanded by Capt. Russell S. Bodfish, then lying at Pier No.—North River.

My "outfit" consisted of several suits of heavy and coarse clothing, including three pairs of "stogy" boots, which, in consideration of that fact that I was yet a "growing" boy, were of graduated sizes; these, with sundry tarpaulin hats, salt-water soap, and many knick-knacks and conveniences which kind friends provided, were packed in a seamen's chest, which during the long voyage also served as my seat at the table.

It was thought prudent to provide against the possibilities of famine, and several barrels of mess-beef, pork and ship biscuit were purchased and shipped on a vessel to follow the *Panama.*

For protection against the wild Indians and wilder Spaniards, with which imagination peopled the land, I provided myself with an "Arsenal" consisting of a double-barreled gun (cost $8.00) with rifled and smooth bore; an Allen's revolver of pepper-box pattern, and a bowie knife of formidable dimensions.

The former weapons served a useful purpose by employing my time on board ship—cleaning and oiling. The revolver was thrown away, soon after my arrival in California, as being more dangerous to the shooter than to the shot-at; the gun, which, through lack of taste for firearms, I had discharged a few times only, provided me with some ready money, when hard-up a few days after I landed, finding sale at $35.00. The bowie knife, alas, was reduced to the ignoble service of carving my meat.

I must not omit to mention as among my outfit a small library of selected books for reading on the voyage; a stoutly bound blank book for my "Log" or Journal, in which, by special understanding with my good cousin Avis, who entered enthusiastically into all my plans and aspirations, every day's events, whether trivial or otherwise, was carefully and faithfully written down; plenty of paper and pens, for I promised to be and was for several years, a faithful correspondent; a Bible, presented to me by my grand-mother on my thirteenth birthday, on the fly-leaf of which I now read: "Ship *Panama* at sea, Sunday, Feb. 11, 1849; commenced with the intention of reading regularly until I read it through," but which the ear-marks make evident that the resolution did not carry me beyond "Exodus"; and my mother's daguerreotype, over which I cried often and bitterly, when suffering from that most distressing of all heart-diseases, "home-sickness."

Thus equipped, I waited impatiently for the sailing of the vessel, which was delayed for various reasons, until January passed away. It was finally announced that we would sail on the 2nd of February, and on the afternoon of the 1st, I went on board and busied myself arranging my "traps." I spent my first night on board and experienced my first home-sickness, which resulted in my returning home again next morning, it being understood that the sailing would be again postponed until the morning of the 3rd.

At nine o'clock of that day I was again on board; preparations were being made for departure; the day was clear and very cold, with a strong north-west wind blowing; passengers and their friends crowded the decks and the wharf; and, as the lines were cast off and the ship moved slowly from the wharf, the former gathered in the rigging, and lustily joined in the then popular refrain, to the tune of "Oh, Susannah!"

"Ho, for California! that's the land for me,
I'm bound for the Sacramento
With my wash-bowl on my knee."

As the ship passed rapidly toward Sandy Hook, I sat upon the taffrail watching the receding city until, with the setting sun glistening the cross of Trinity Church, as it sank below the horizon, I saw the last of my boyhood's home, and thought how long in the future seemed then *three years* which must intervene before I should return to it; that the time would be longer, did not then seem possible.

Just *twenty-three* (less one month) actually did elapse before, crossing the North River, via the Pennsylvania Railroad through City, I again entered New York.

Thus, "The best laid plans of mice and men
Gang aft aglee."

The first day after our sailing was Sunday, and the Episcopal Service was read; nearly all the passengers attended, as the wind being favorable and the ship steady, few had yet experienced the qualms of seasickness.

This gave us an opportunity also to examine the quarters, which were to be our home for so many months, and to make the acquaintance of those whose enforced companionship we were to enjoy with more or less satisfaction.

The *Panama* was a full rigged ship of — tons burthen, formerly in the China Sea trade, purchased and fitted up for this voyage by an Association, a share of which entitled the holder to California, and a home in the vessel while lying in the harbor of San Francisco, or "at the mines," as the Association might determine on arrival.

If I remember rightly, there were, all told, including officers and crew, 220 souls on board. Of these, four were women; the Captain and First Mate had each their wives, and there were two lady passengers, a Mrs. Leavett, accompanying her husband, and a Mrs. M. E. Longley, a widow of thirty-eight or forty years. All these occupied state-rooms in the house on deck, eating at the Captain's table. The rest of the passengers were young men, with very few exceptions, under thirty years of age; for their accommodation, the space "between decks" from stem to stern was fitted up, through the entire length on each side, with wide bunks one above the other, each capable of holding two persons with tolerable comfort; a table ran lengthwise through this space, which by courtesy was called "The Saloon"; racks above the table held such dishes as were not needed in the pantry, and slats along the table prevented the plates, etc., from slipping about in rough weather. On each side of this long table, and ranging along the fronts of the berths, were our sea-chests and trunks serving for seats. Whale oil lamps (these were days before petroleum and coal oil were discovered) here and there suspended from the ceiling, shed a dim, uncertain light during the night, or when the hatches were closed and battened down off the stormy Cape.

One of the rules of the Association made it necessary to select our berths by lot, so it happened that a Mr. Martin became my berth-mate; this gentleman was about ten years my elder; an Artist and a Bohemian, a *bon-vivant*, whose sea-chest was filled with choice cigars and liquors, which rendered the neighborhood of his berth a favorite resort fór the "good fellows" on board. I remember well a small keg, which occupied a central portion of the chest, with a flexible rubber syphon attachment to draw out the contents; my firm temperance principles prevented me from participating in it, nor was I ever fully in sympathy with the games of cards, which seemed of interminable length, during the days and nights when stormy weather kept all hands below deck.

By Monday (third day out) we ran into the gulf stream, where the uneasy cross-seas brought the landsmen to a full realization of the nature of sea-sickness. I will not attempt a description of it, but I remember well the utter disregard of life or care for the future, as I lay upon the deck or reached limply over the side "paying tribute to Neptune." Remembering the advice of good, old Captain Coffin, I had, as soon as the first qualmish feeling manifested itself, obtained some warm water from the ocean, and drinking copiously of this, not only aggravated the retching but hastened the reaction and cure.

Two days after, I had materially recovered, and could enjoy my meals with tolerable comfort; many, however, were for several days afterward still under its influence, and one elderly gentleman did not fully recover as long as we were at sea. We were not many weeks out on our voyage, before complaints were active concerning the quality and quantity of the food which was served us. I now know that such complaints are almost universal under similar circumstances, but it then appeared to me as though we were especially [deprived], and I was very ready and willing to join in the denunciation of those who had provisioned the ship, and sent us to sea without an abundance of those things which on shore are deemed essential to comfort and health.

These complaints reached the proper authorities, who caused an investigation to be made of the ship's stores, which developed the fact, that while there was an apparent abundance of beef, bread and the more substantial articles, there was a very meagre supply of butter, sugar, rice and similar provisions, and this resulted in apportioning to each passenger a certain "allowance"; for this purpose, the passengers were divided into messes of ten, each of which selected its steward, who received the allowance for his mess: to still further systematize matters, a "bill of fare" for the week was prepared, and this system continued with but little interruption, except by the occasional failure of some articles, until the end of the voyage.

While the sailing of the ship was left altogether to the Captain and his officers, the affairs of the Association were under the control of a Board of Directors, who, if my memory serves me aright, were elected monthly; these elections added life and interest to the trip, causing a diversion in the monotony of the voyage, local events being made the issues, and the success of the candidates dependent upon their willingness and ability to institute reforms in our "cuisine." The bulletin-board which was placed in front of the cabin on deck, was placarded with the rallying cries: "Pensam! and no lob-scouse"; "Vote for Whitman! and more soft-tack," etc., with caricatures from the pencils of the artists on board.

The incidents of the voyage were probably not unlike those on every other vessel similarly occupied and on a similar voyage; we rarely spoke or sighted other vessels; there were two notable exceptions which made impression on my memory; on one occasion we had a fair breeze (not equal to the best capacity of our ship) when far off in the horizon, astern, appeared the topmasts of a single masted vessel, as the hours passed she gained steadily on us, until finally she danced alongside and her crew came on board; she appeared like a mere atom on the waste of waters, and I could hardly realize that she dared to venture so far on the vast ocean. She proved to be a pilot-boat bought and worked by a crew of New York Pilots on their way to California. She passed through the Straits of Magellan, arrived safely at her destination, took her passengers well up the Sacramento and American Rivers, and was subsequently placed in the pilot service.

On another occasion we spoke the ship *Borneo*, ninety-three days from Calcutta, bound for London, and had an opportunity to put on board a bag of letters. These I subsequently learned were carried to England and deposited in a post-office; being without stamps for the postage to America, official notice was sent to several addresses that on receipt of the proper postage, the letters would be forwarded. In my own home, this official communication created a great deal of speculation, and the mystery grew as the days passed until the letters by sea arrived.

We soon ran into warmer latitudes, and as we neared and passed the Equator, the constellations of the Southern Hemisphere, new to Northern eyes, came into view; conspicuous among them, being the Southern Cross, the mysterious Clouds of Magellan, etc.

Reading, writing, the inevitable card playing, lounging about the decks in fair weather, cleaning and repairing guns and pistols, occupied the time.

Early in April we began to get a foretaste of Cape Horn by much rough weather, and when the sailors sent down the topmasts, and otherwise put the ship in condition to encounter the storms which continually hold high carnival around the Icy Cape, there was a very decided longing for terra-firma in the minds of many who were making their first sea voyage.

On the sixth of April (our 62nd day out) we were off the Falkland

Islands, and now began to experience a succession of south-westerly gales, which carried us as far south as latitude 58 30', about 200 miles south of the Cape. One of my old letters, briefly describing the voyage, says: "We were thirty days in doubling the Cape, during this time we had gale after gale—nearly all the time *lying to* with the hatches battened, and all hands below."

A picture painted on board by Mr. James J. Ayres, an excellent Marine Artist, fitly represents the ship as she appeared in the grand gale of the sixteenth of April. A photographic copy of this picture (the original of which is in the possession of the family of Captain Bodfish) is one of my most valued souvenirs of the voyage. Mr. Ayres was lost in the foundering of the Schooner *Ocean Pearl*, on the northern coast, while on voyage to study marine effects. At length we cleared Cape Victory at the entrance of the Straits of Magellan, on the Pacific, and had thus actually "doubled the Cape." Among the amusements, during the weather which permitted us to remain on deck, was "fishing" for Albatross; this was done by baiting a shark hook with a piece of pork, and this being fastened to a bit of wood, was towed astern by a strong rope; the bird seeing it, was caught in his hooked bill, which his efforts to escape only caused to cling tighter to the hook, and he was drawn on board. They are of beautiful plumage, perfectly white, and exceedingly graceful as they rest upon the water, but awkward and unsteady when placed on deck, from which they cannot arise without assistance. One that I caught in this manner, measured ten feet six inches from tip to tip of his wings when spread.

With warmer weather came renewed spirits; we were now on the "home stretch," and every day's sailing took us nearer our goal, and we should speedily know for ourselves, if these things were so; if our long voyage was to end in disappointment, or if the news which had impelled us was indeed true. Plans for future guidance in California were discussed, partnerships formed—all based upon actual mining operations; the deck in fair weather was transformed into a workshop, where gold-rockers, tents, etc., were made.

We had now been three months at sea, during which time we had seen nothing but a monotonous waste of waters, and had been subjected to as monotonous a diet of the usual ship stores. We began to long for and speculate upon a landing; Juan Fernandez, off the coast of Chili, appealed to our romantic imaginations as the most desirable point to be visited, and we pictured to ourselves the delights of a ramble among the caves and groves, so long the home of Robinson Crusoe; that Robinson was a myth gave us no anxiety whatever. But the fact that the ship was greatly in need of supplies, of which the continent furnished a better market, determined those in authority to land at one of the ports on the coast of Chili, and the ship's head was turned in that direction.

On the fifteenth day of May (our 101st day out) we heard the cheering sound of Land Ho! which brought every one on deck. Far away on the horizon appeared what to me seemed a low bank of clouds, but which the Captain said was the Island of Mocha; we kept along the coast until the eighteenth day of May, when we made the Island of Santa Maria. At this juncture an accident occurred, which came near ending me and my aspirations altogether.

I have already mentioned that every Californian had furnished himself with an outfit of guns and pistols, and that cleaning these furnished much relief from the monotony of the voyage; in preparation for use on shore, these were now brought out, cleaned and discharged, the sea-gulls and other aquatic birds furnishing fair targets; a friend had prepared to discharge his gun at a distant gull, and I was seated near by watching intently to see the effect of the shot; suddenly a blinding discharge, and a stinging blow toppled me from my seat, and for a few hours I was unconscious. When I recovered, I found myself in the cabin, with the surgeon probing a wound in my left temple; the gun had bursted at the breech, and the nipple had struck me sufficiently near the temple to leave a most uncomfortable wound, with no permanent effects, however, except to leave a scar.

We ran rapidly along the coast, and soon sighted the Island of Quirikina at the entrance of the Bay of Talcahuano; the main channel runs north of this Island, passing through which we came into a handsome bay, and anchored amid a small fleet of American vessels, like ourselves bound California-ward, which had come into this port to recruit.

The large number of passengers on our ship, and our Brass Band organized among them, which discoursed patriotic airs as we passed along, attracted to us more than usual attention, and we were soon visited by many boats—some with curiosity to know who and whence we were, others to earn a few "reals" in carrying the eager passengers ashore. None, of course, were permitted to board the ship, nor were we permitted to go on shore until the Commandante del Puerto, or Custom-House Officer, came on board and vised our papers, which being found in order, a permit was given.

The Brig *Osceola*, from Philadelphia, with passengers, had cast anchor a few days before in the Bay DeChatta, a short distance south of the proper Bay, and some of the impatient passengers had landed and made their way to Talcahuano, ignorant or unmindful of the laws of the port. The brig was ready to sail, and the passengers were impatient to proceed on their voyage, but the authorities, secretly aided and abetted it was thought by the American Consul, refused to give them clearance papers; several of those who were first to visit us, were of this brig, and they appealed to us to help them in their extremity, so that almost before we had made a landing, arrangements were made for a "mass meeting" in front of the Custom House or principal hotel, of the Americans in port, "to take into consideration the outrageous proceedings toward the brig *Osceola*"; whether the notice had the desired effect, or negotiations had already reached favorable conclusions, I do not know, but the papers were soon thereafter forthcoming, and the *Osceola* proceeded to sea.

This diversion, however, carries me a little ahead of my story.

It may be readily understood, that as soon as the Captain of the Port had given his permission, we lost no time in going ashore, and once more set our feet on terra-firma.

The town of Talcahuano was then a straggling village, picturesquely situated on a slope extending to the water's edge; with scarcely an exception it was made up of one story buildings built of adobe, with thatched and tiled roofs. It numbered about three thousand inhabitants. About thirteen years previously (in 1836) the old town was thrown down by an earthquake, which also destroyed the city of Concepcion ten miles distant; a huge tidal wave swept far up the slope, and, it was said, the shore line settled and did not resume its old position. We were told that the old walls could be seen at the bottom of the bay, but we had no ocular demonstration of this. A few of the houses had tiled floors, but in the main the ground was bare, with very little furniture, one invariable item of which was a brazier of charcoal burning in the center.

The Custom-House, also used as a hotel by an enterprising American, was an exception, being of two stories with piazzas extending around each story—in front and on the sides; this, also the church or cathedral, and calaboose or jail, faced the Plaza or Public Square, which is a conspicuous feature in all Spanish towns, and to this we directed our steps, and were soon surrounded by passengers from the other ships, some of which had been in port for several days and were preparing to resume their journey. We quickly fraternized, and, although from all parts of the Union, no sectional differences divided us, for we were united under one flag, and knew but one name—Americans.

There were, perhaps, six hundred California-bound persons in port; of the vessels bringing them, I remember the names of the brig *Osceola*, from Philadelphia; ship *Albany*, from New York; ships *Trescott* and *Lenore*, bark *Oxford*, and brig *Mary Wilder*, from Boston; brig *Charlotte*, from Newburyport, Mass.; ship *Hopewell*, from Warren, R.I.; bark *Diamond* from New Bedford, Mass.; and, brig *John Petty*, from Norfolk, VA.

Through these we learned that many vessels had gone from Chili to California, and that the gold fever was as active in the Spanish American towns as in the Atlantic cities of our own Country.

I remember that we met a man who professed to have been to "the mines," who was always the center of a group of open-mouthed, anxious gold-hunters, who appeared to place implicit faith in all his statements as to the wonders of the region to which we were bound. At this distance of time, I am prepared to believe that he was simply an adventurer, such as may always be found in such places, and under similar circumstances, ready to respond to the invitations to imbibe the "Aguadiente" given in exchange for his recitals.

The passengers of the *Panama* had adopted a uniform, consisting of a red shirt turned down over a white shirt; black pants and leather belt, and California hats, turned up on the side. This uniform, with our Brass Band, made us a conspicuous feature, and as we were more numerous than those of any other ship, added much to the picturesqueness of the groups.

There was much to interest us in the town; so different in every particular from those of our own Country—the narrow, irregular and unpaved streets, the unfloored houses, the numerous "burros," or donkeys, (the only beasts of burden,) no less than the Chilenos themselves being objects of interest.

The people were very hospitable, and the Californians were, as a rule, welcome guests; although many rudely trespassed upon their hospitality; the cup of Mate, or Paraguay Tea, was freely offered to those who did not take kindly to the fiery "Aguadiente." The lack of knowledge of the Spanish language on our part was an obstruction to free conversations; but I managed, with the help of Ollendorf's Phrase Book; to pick up a few words and sentences during my stay, which helped me materially. I have often wondered if the little Chilian girl, at whose house I was always made welcome, who sympathized with my bandaged head, ever gave a thought after we sailed, to Jorge, (pronounced Horka,) who carried a "Medio" attached to his watch chain, in exchange for an American copper cent, as a keepsake.

We fairly reveled in the luxuries of fresh bread, cheese, chocolate, apples and green vegetables, compensating for the deprivation of these articles on ship-board. With an eye to the future, I laid in a supply of the least perishable goods, and filled the vacant spaces in my sea-chest with apples, potatoes, etc., the latter to be eaten raw as a preventive of scurvy; the few dollars ($35 in all) which were left after the payment of my passage, outfit, etc., converted into dimes and carefully kept in a buckskin bag, were all left in Talcahuano in exchange for these commodities.

A few days after our arrival, an excursion was planned to the city of Concepcion, nine or ten miles distant; assembling on the Plaza, in front of the hotel or Custom-House, we found a large number of Chilenos, with their diminutive donkeys, caparisoned with their peculiar sheepskin saddles, in readiness for hire to the Americanos whose purses or ambition permitted to make the journey mounted. Being inexperienced in such matters, the choicer beasts (if there was any choice) were secured before I had made my selection, which finally and perforce settled upon a small jackass of remarkable length of ears, and wonderful lung power, as evidenced by his stentorian bray. Across this beast were strapped sundry layers of sheepskins over a peculiar saddle tree, having a high pommel "fore and aft," and huge blocks of wood for stirrups; to mount this I was assisted by the owner, and then my troubles had just commenced; the Spanish bit and the manner of using it were entirely new to me; the huge and jingling spurs proved instruments of torment to the beast, as I unintentionally thrust them into his sides; rebelling against the unwonted pulling or jerks upon the barbarous Spanish bits, the jack alternated between a crouching position on his haunches or frantic pawings in the air, in the midst of which, by convulsively clinging to forward pommel, I managed to keep my seat. By signs and gestures, the master of the "burro" made me understand that he must be driven with an entirely slack rein, the direction to be given by tapping or pressing the rein on the side of the neck opposite to that in which it was desired the beast should go, and that his usual gait was a "lope" or gallop.

After these explanations, with a peculiar whoop! my animal was started, his desire to overtake his companions, now a mile or more in advance, being encouraged by the murderous spurs which my helpless legs kept plunging into his sides—helpless, because a new and over-large pair of stogy boots, put on in honor of the occasion, would insist upon working off by the pressure of the toes in the block stirrup, which did not permit more than an inch or so to be inserted. In sheer desperation, I allowed the stirrups to dangle, and as best I could, clung with my knees to the sheepskin saddle, to avoid the unmerciful pounding on the projecting pommel in the rear.

In this plight, at full gallop, I at length overtook some of our tourists who were making the trip afoot, and gladly dismounted or was helped to dismount, giving my steed to one of them, and finished the journey in that primitive style, a wiser and sorer man—or boy.

We found Concepcion to be a well laid out city of about fifteen thousand inhabitants, one-eighth of whom were said to be Europeans and Americans; it is situated on the bank of the Biobio River, about ten miles from its mouth, and is built on a gently sloping plain, surrounded on three sides by high hills.

As in Talcahuano, the houses are of one story because of the liability to earthquakes; I think there were two exceptions, the cathedral and the residence of the Governor, which are above one story.

In 1836, the entire city, with the exception of three houses, was destroyed by an earthquake. There were many wealthy people in Concepcion, because of its position as the Capitol of the province, and in consequence, there were many elegant homes.

While writing, I have had the curiosity to consult the Cyclopaedia, to ascertain what changes have been brought about in Concepcion and Talcahuano since my visit thirty years ago, through the introduction of railroads, telegraphs, and other modern civilizers. "Appleton's" says of Concepcion: "It is a well-built city, with wide streets crossing at right angles. Near the center is a square with a fine fountain. Among the principal buildings is a handsome cathedral; a number of churches and free schools; an orphan asylum; a lyceum; theatre; prison; hospital; and, barracks. It is the seat of a Bishop. Its port, Talcahuano, about twelve miles distant, on the south-west side of Concepcion Bay, is one of the best in Chili. It has been rebuilt entirely since the earthquake of 1835, and now contains about five thousand inhabitants, and a number of churches and schools. A railway from Talcahuano to Chillan (112 miles) now constructing, will materially increase its importance. Concepcion was founded by Pedro Valdivia in 1550, on the south side of the bay. It was burned by the Araucanians several times, and suffered severely from earthquakes. After the earthquake in 1751, it was rebuilt on its present site. In 1823, the Araucanians again destroyed a part of it, and it was nearly ruined by the earthquake of 1835."

After a day spent in rambling through the city, we returned to Talcahuano. There was a general impression among us, that the Chilians were treacherous and vindictive; that they were especially hostile to the "Californians," and lost no opportunity, when one of the latter could be found alone, to rob or murder him; we had been especially advised before leaving, that the desperado lurked among the chaparral, en route, prepared to spring out and "lasso" the stragglers. We therefore kept closely together, in groups, prepared to make good use of our revolvers, should we meet any of these gentry.

We met a number of [Chilians] mounted on ponies, with lassos hanging over the horns of their saddles, whose countenances indicated their ability to commit almost any murderous deed, but we were not molested.

A fierce norther was blowing when we reached Talcahuano, so that it was not thought prudent to return to the ship, and a large number of us, who could not be accommodated with beds at the hotel, and were not disposed to wrestle with the fleas, and other discomforts at the "fandango" houses, made a night of it on the reception room carpet, where, tired, stiff and sore, I tossed uneasily until morning.

We remained three weeks in port; at this distance of time, I cannot remember the cause of delay, but I know that we became very impatient, and that much dissatisfaction was expressed with those who were responsible for it.

At length the welcome information was given that we would sail on the morrow, and on the —— day of June, 1849, we hove anchor, and, with flags flying, and band playing, all the passengers being assembled on deck in their red shirt uniform, we led the way out of the harbor, our companions being the "*Hopewell*" and "*Cristoval Colon*."

The usual routine of sea-life was soon resumed; the weather in the Pacific was more gentle that we had experienced in the Atlantic; we had more calms, and these tested our patience to the uttermost; for days at a time we lay, with sails flapping against the masts, the sun pouring down on us from a cloudless sky, "as idle as a painted ship upon a painted ocean."

Advantage was taken of these calms to clean, fit, and paint the ship, preparatory to reaching San Francisco, which event we still hoped was not far distant, when favorable winds should carry us into the north-east trades.

A favorite pastime, during these days, was catching Cape Pigeons, or speckled Haglets, a bird about the size of a large pigeon, of beautiful plumage; these surrounded our ship in large numbers, attracted, perhaps, by the offal thrown out from the cook's galley, over which as it floated by and astern of the ship, they would keep up a loud chattering; to catch these, we would suspend small ropes or strings over the sides, allowing them to float to the surface; a handful of "slush" would then be thrown overboard from the bows, and, in their struggles for these morsels, the birds would become entangled in the lines, and could be hauled on board—frequently three or four birds on a single string. Once on deck, like the Albatross, they had no ability to raise themselves, and lost the grace of motion which characterized them, when on the wave or on the wing.

The Cape Pigeon furnished us a change of diet, and under the manipulations of the cook, with sufficient par-boiling to take away the fishy taste, our pigeon pot-pies were not an indifferent substitute for the land article.

Midsummer found us nearer the Equator, which we again crossed on the third day of July.

The Fourth of July was approaching, and, as patriotic Americans, we must give it appropriate recognition; with characteristic manner, a "mass-meeting" was called, pursuant to notice posted on the "Bulletin Board," the official organ of the ship; at this, a committee of arrangement was appointed.

The day was ushered in by a salute of thirteen guns from our little cannon, as the flag was run to the masthead; the ship was fully decoraed with all the available signal and other flags. At noon a salute was fired of thirty guns, one for each of the States then composing the American Union. Throughout the day, at frequent intervals, volunteer salutes, with gun and pistol, furnished the necessary noise and smell of powder, sufficient to satisfy the most exacting "Young American" on the ship. Early in the afternoon all hands were assembled on deck, in the front of the cabin, where the usual anniversary exercises were had: Prayer by the "Chaplain"; Reading of the Declaration of Independence; an Oration; Drake's Address to the American Flag; and an original poem by our "learned Blacksmith"; interspersed by patriotic airs by the Brass Band.

If we were far away from our homes, we did not forget that we were yet part of the Great Republic; yet few thought, nor did our orator prophecy, that the land to which we were journeying, the youngest of our Country's Acquisitions, would soon be enrolled among the "States"—one of the most important in the constellation. At the dinner which followed the exercises, the cooks exhausted their larders in the efforts to do justice to the occasion, and an extra allowance of "plum-duff" was served, to which an occasional fortunate passenger gave his portion zest, by the addition of a flavor of brandy or wine, to his "hard sauce" worked up from his carefully husbanded allowance of butter and sugar.

The evening was devoted to a Fancy Dress Ball; think of it,—only four women on board, and only one with the taste or inclination to dance; yet we had a ball, and the fun was unbounded.

The costumes were as varied as the tastes and opportunities of the wearers; the lack of lady partners being made up by the substitution of the younger, and smoother-faced gentlemen, in calico gowns. Thanks to Mrs. Longley, I was made presentable as a young lady, and though I could not dance I could manage to walk through the figures and was, in consequence, in active demand. I remember among the absurd costumes, that of our stalwart second mate—six feet high in his stockings—as "Mrs. Partington," with a little man, one of the oldest on board, in short jacket and trousers, as "Ike." These festivities were carried far into the night, and so closed, on the ship *Panama*, the Fourth of July, 1849.

And now we began to look anxiously for the end of our voyage. Over five months had passed since we set sail, and we began to make calculations as to the probable day when we should set our feet in California. The long confinement and indifferent food had become irksome, and great efforts were required to prevent petty bickerings and quarreling; old arrangements were broken up; new partnerships were formed, and new plans for mining and trading enterprises were entered into. As for myself, the future, and my own plans in connection with it, were very indefinite. The "mines" were, of course, the objective point, but where they were, or how mining was prosecuted, I do not think I had formed an idea. I can only recall now a determination to do my best with whatever came to hand. In this spirit we approached the latitude of San Francisco and began to get indications of the land, a principal one being the prevalence of heavy fogs, which then, as now, hung along the coast during July and August. We began also to meet an occasional vessel, pointed like ourselves toward the Golden Gate. From one of these, the brig *Orion*, on the twenty-eighth of July, we took four American passengers in a destitute condition, and also supplied her with sails and water. This vessel had been one hundred and forty-five days out from Valparaiso for California; had put into Acapulco, on the coast of Mexico, whence she had taken the Americans, who had made their way to the coast through Mexico. The prevalence of fogs kept us from "taking the sun," and thus finding the entrance to the harbor for several days. There were no pilots in those days, and we had to rely upon the nautical skill of Captain Bodfish, and his mates, to carry us in safely.

For a few days before we reached the entrance to the harbor, a sharp look-out had to be kept up, not only for the breakers, but for other vessels. I remember that early in the evening of the seventh of August, as I sat on the taffrail at the stern of the vessel, peering out into the fog, there suddenly loomed up a dark and shadowy object of immense size, magnified, perhaps, by the fog and indistinctness. She passed quickly across our stern and disappeared almost as suddenly as she had appeared; neither ship hailed the other, but from the glimpse we got of her build, we thought it was the British ship which the next day hailed us for information as to our reckoning, and for which we acted as pilot, as she followed closely in our wake into the harbor.

And now the sun rose on the last day of our long and eventful voyage; all our mutterings ceased and our discontent ended; apologies for harsh words said and unkind things done were exchanged; compliments were voted to our officers for their skill and success in bringing us safely through. There was much cause for gratitude to Almighty God that our voyage had been safely made; that death had not lessened our numbers; and, that serious sickness had not visited us. There was no public recognition of this feeling, but I have no doubt that it was shared by many; my journal chronicles it as my own belief.

Creeping slowly along through the fog, which occasionally lifted or became thin, we first made land, as I now remember it, at Helmet Rock, so called from its shape. Thus getting our bearings we passed rapidly eastward through the Golden Gate; as we entered, the fog entirely lifted and the sun shone out brightly, giving us a cheering welcome. On our left the brown hills back of Saucelito were dotted with cattle; on our right we noticed an earthwork fortification, with dismantled guns pointing towards the channel. Followed closely by the British ship referred to, with flags flying and band playing, we passed up the channel, rounded Clark's Point, and at about six o'clock on the afternoon of the *eighth day of August*, 1894, cast anchor opposite the cove, on the slopes of which were located the tents and shanties then constituting the infant City of San Francisco.

Every man was on deck and straining his eyes to gather in the strange scenes before him. Nearly every man was in his "uniform" of red shirt, and this, with our Band, making us conspicuous among the many vessels which daily dropped anchor from all parts of the world, attracted a number of small boats; in the leading one some of our passengers recognized an old acquaintance—"Commodore" Robert Martin—and this colloquy ensued, which, being the first interchange of salutations between ship and shore, became fixed in my memory:

"Hallo, Bob! What's the news?"
"Plenty of gold, but hard to get it!"

And thus were the reports confirmed to us. The men from the boats soon came on board, and speedily formed the nuclei of eager passengers, hungry for information concerning the city, the mines, and the news from "the States," for it will be remembered that one hundred and eighty-six days had passed since we had heard a word of what had transpired in the world at large. Outside of our own little community on shipboard, the world had been to us a blank for over six months. They brought us the leading events from the Atlantic States up to within thirty days of the time of which I am now writing. Of California news, I can only remember how I drank in, open-mouthed, all that they said, so much of which sounded like romance; my head whirled and my brain tired in the effort to grasp it all; there was no sleep for me, but I sat on the taffrail, watching the glimmer of the lights as they shone through the many tents of which the city was then largely made up. Toward midnight, those of our passengers who had gone ashore returned in the ship's boats, and these were obliged to tell again and again of the strange scenes they had encountered in their visit.

The next morning Mr. Tucker and I went ashore. Our first landing in California was made among the rocks, which formed a portion of the north arm of the cove, in which the town lay, called Clark's Point; adjoining the place where we landed had been built a short wharf—the only one. The cove I have alluded to, formed a graceful curve, the water at high tide reaching nearly to Montgomery Street; the southern end was then, as now, called Rincon Point. The most southerly street of the town was California Street, and on this but a few straggling houses and cloth-covered frames had been built. South of this, sand hills, covered with scrub oaks and chaparral, occupied the site, and on these, extending to the bay, were hundreds of tents, the locality being called "Happy Valley." The principal streets, extending east and west, were Vallejo, Jackson, Washington, Clay, Commercial, Sacramento and California—in this order commencing on the north. Montgomery Street was the farthest east, running north and south; then Kearney, Dupont, Stockton and Powell; other streets were mapped out, but there were scarcely houses enough to distinguish, the tents and shanties extending irregularly along the trails or over the hills, as caprice and convenience dictated. There were no paved streets, no planking, no sidewalks. A large proportion of the people were living in tents, or in cloth-stretched frames. Some of the more pretentious houses and business places were constructed of boards taken from packing boxes. With lumber worth from four hundred to five hundred dollars per thousand feet, everything had to be utilized. There were no wharves running to deep water, and the vessels, many without keepers (the crews having deserted and gone to the mines) were anchored in the bay, in some instances serving as boarding-houses. It is remarkable, that notwithstanding the fact that many of the ships which made the voyage in '49 were old hulks, not a few few of them so old that they would never had made another voyage, but for the extraordinary demand of the gold excitement, all arrived in safety, although some, by reason of their clumsy build, made extraordinary long passages, and in some instances losing many of their passengers by scurvy, by reason of their long deprivations.

Of the arrivals by water in 1849, a historian says: "In April, two vessels arrived from the Atlantic, having started in November, 1848. In May, only one came; in June, eleven; in July, forty; in August, forty-three; in September, sixty-six; in October, twenty-eight; in November, twenty-three; and in December, nineteen; a total of two hundred and thirty-three in nine months. In addition to these, three hundred and sixteen vessels arrived in that period from other ports, making a total of five hundred and forty-nine arrivals, and an average of two vessels a day. The passengers of the year arriving by sea numbered thirty-five thousand, including twenty-three thousand Americans."

Our first visit, like that of every new comer, was to the Post Office, which we found in a low, broad-eaved building of one story, on the corner of Clay and Pike streets—now Waverley Place. We received the long and anxiously looked for letters from our friends; not the least, in importance, was one to me from Mr. Turney, written three months previously at Mormon Island, on the North Fork of the American River, whither he had gone on his arrival in May, and was then engaged in mining. He advised me to sell my supplies and come up there, but mentioned that I would get other advices from him by inquiry of G. B. Post, merchant.

To Mr. Post, therefore, we went, and there found that Mr. Turney had returned from the mines, and was then employed as book-keeper for Francis Salmon & Co., merchants, on Pacific Street. Mr. Turney related his experience to us, that he had enough of mining and was then contemplating an early return to the States. While conversing with him, Mr. Salmon accosted me and asked me if I desired work and could paint a wagon box. I made no hesitancy in responding aye to the former interrogatory, but had some misgivings as to my ability to do the latter, never having handled a brush or mixed paints. On Mr. Tucker's advice (he was by trade a carpenter) who volunteered to prepare the paint, I accepted the job; the bargain was made, and in due time the wagon was painted, and I earned my first money ($5.00) in California.

I have no doubt that the incident was of advantage to me, beyond the mere receipt of the money, as it gave me courage to believe that I had something more than mere clerical ability.

For several days we made our home on board the *Panama*, coming ashore in the morning and returning at night in the ship's boats, meanwhile looking about for a temporary location, and such odd jobs as would pay the way, until my "supplies" arrived, and we could go to "the mines," which charmed localities, notwithstanding many adverse reports, were, until the advent of the rainy season, the objective point of our desires.

The largest proportion of the adventurers, who were arriving daily by hundreds, were encamping in tents and shelters of brush, in and about Happy Valley, which occupied the eastern slopes of the sand hills, south of California Street, extending to the bay shore, but the members of our party selected a beautiful valley in the hills back of the town, abounding in scrubby oaks and chaparral, about where the blocks bounded by Clay, Jackson, Mason and Powell Streets now lie; a fine spring in the neighborhood furnished us with delicious water. This spring, I understand, is the original of the Spring Valley Water Company, which now furnishes the City of San Francisco with water, and the modern Legislatures with lobby delegates for its regulation.

At Mrs. Longley's request, I assisted her in erecting a shelter of branches of trees and twigs, covered in part with tent cloth; this furnished two rooms, by a partition of like materials. One of these served as a general eating and living room, and the other as a bedroom for Mrs. Longley. The bedsteads were of small branches of trees, slightly raised above the ground, interwoven with ropes. The house being prepared, our traps were removed from the ship, and Mrs. Longley kept boarding-house, a number of our fellow-passengers boarding with her.

Before parting company in these pages with Mrs. Longley, I ought to say that she was a woman of a great deal of energy and enterprise, who had come to California to make money, and meant to do it. Before settling down into regular boarding-house ways, she proposed to me to join her in the laundry business, as she had heard that washing commanded nine dollars per dozen pieces; that she would do the manual labor at the wash-tub and ironing-board, and I should furnish the capital represented by the firewood, also receive and deliver the articles to be manipulated. As this enterprise was as promising as anything else, I accepted, but the copartnership was dissolved in about ten days, as the high price of cord-wood (about $20) precluded much "dividends" to my share, and there was, moreover, a lack of adaptability to the requirements of the position on my own part.

Mrs. Longley received proposals of marriage very soon after her settlement in California, from a Mr. Gingery, who was encamped near us. He was somewhat advanced in years, a Pioneer of Pioneers, who was with Sutter when gold was discovered, and reputed to be wealthy; as he had no intellectual or physical recommendations, and she had long passed the period of youthful "gush," the Camp agreed that love did not enter into the disposing causes, but a more sordid impulse, at least on her part, influenced her course. We learned that the marriage was not a happy one. The couple subsequently went to the mines; I heard of her a few years thereafter from one who had met her on one of the bars of the Yuba. Mr. Gingery had taken a contract to build a road, when he mysteriously disappeared.

A few words here of the old ship which had been our home for so many months; like many others which arrived during the Summer and Fall of 1849, she was almost abandoned, officers and crews generally going to the mines, or more lucrative employments on shore. A few months after our arrival, the *Panama* was sold to Macondry & Co., who used her as a warehouse, and subsequently sold her to a Seamens' Bethel Organization; she was hauled up onto the flats in front of the city, to a place now represented by the corner of Sacramento and Davis Streets, and concerted into a church. In one of my trips from the mountains in the Fall of 1852, I visited the old vessel; the filling in of the streets, which had already commenced for the purpose of reclaiming the entire area between Clark's and Rincon Points, had progressed so far, that almost solid earth constituted Sacramento Street to the old ship; a large doorway had been cut in her side, through which I entered the space between-decks which constituted our living place during the voyage, this had been fitted up with rude seats or pews, the berths had been removed and a pulpit erected at the stern.

My initials carved on one of the deck beams, over the place where my berth had been, was the only record about her, of my connection with the *Panama*.

She was, I believe, subsequently burned, in one of the fires which so often swept away the city during the early years.

Our Captain (Mr. Bodfish) and his family settled in Coloma, where gold was discovered.

With this digression I take up the narrative of the early weeks. Without any fixed ideas as to future movements, except that I should go to the mines, I turned my hands to any employment that offered.

I was offered a position as light porter and clerk by Messrs. Salmon & Co., with a salary of $100 per month and board, but a desire to act upon my own account and a belief that I could utilize my time to better purpose caused me to decline the offer.

My success in painting the wagon directed my efforts towards sign painting. Mr. Tucker had erected a large tent on the southerly slope of Telegraph Hill, facing Montgomery Street, in which he did carpenter work, including the manufacture of pine coffins. For him I painted my first signs on drilling—"Carpenter" for one end, and "Undertaker" for the other, of the tent; the latter occupation gave me an opportunity to put my facilities with the pencil brush to use, in this way: One of our fellow-passengers had been appointed a sort of Acting Coroner under Malichi Fallon, of New York (who was Chief of Police appointed by the Alcade, John W. Geary), and through him Mr. Tucker furnished the city with coffins for the dead who were buried by the city; for such as left a record of their names, or had friends to direct the work, I painted a wooden slab, or mortuary tablet; and up to the time of the removal of the bodies from Yerba Buena Cemetery, which is the site of the new City Hall and the now famous "Sand Lots," some of my early work with "Sacred to the Memory of," etc., was among the decaying memorials in that burial ground.

From painting "gravestones" to painting signs the transition was easy, and as a kindred occupation I added that of lining and papering houses, as occasion permitted.

While doing an irregular business at this sort of work, I encountered an old New York acquaintance, a few years older than myself, Thomas Goin. I found, after the usual greetings and salutations, that he was the proprietor of the Excelsior Restaurant, on Vallejo Street, east of Montgomery. A few words of invitation only were necessary to induce me to take up my abode with him, in capacity of "assistant," and for a while I learned to "labor and wait" on his tables, putting in the spare time at my easel.

The dining room of the establishment was on the second floor, the lower story being fitted up with rows of shelves or bunks, for lodgers, where accommodations were served at one dollar per night; my impression is that the applicants were required to furnish their own blankets. Be this as it may, it frequently happened that lodgers would introduce those unpleasant parasites, which every early Californian so well remembers.

These possibilities led me to prefer a bedstead, extemporized from the dining room chairs, during the month of my stay at the Excelsior Restaurant.

At the end of this time, the lease held by Goin having terminated, the building was leased for a hospital. On the premises adjoining the main building had been built a substantial oven, as a part of the kitchen establishment of the restaurant; the baker-in-chief was a pleasant gentleman, named Bradford, with whom I speedily struck up an arrangement to run the bakery on shares; a considerable portion of my duties in the business of the copartnership consisted in delivering pies to customers, principally among the tents in Happy Valley; our outfit for delivery purposes did not include a horse and wagon, so the only method was on foot and en panier. A couple of champagne baskets, fitted with handles, were the receptacles, each capable of holding a dozen pies; with one of these baskets on each arm, I trudged along, picking my way through the muddy streets, for the rainy season had already set in. This proved fairly lucrative, and lasted several weeks, until Mr. Bradford's departure for the mines made it necessary that our partnership should come to an end, and I to some other occupation.

As I have mentioned, the rainy season had set in, and the memorable Winter of '49 was upon us; few were prepared for its severity; the frail houses and tents were no proof against the down-pour.

The streets, especially Montgomery (the principal avenue), became deep sloughs of mud, through which men and animals struggled—jokes concerning the disappearance of an ox-team here, or the indifference of a mounted man there, who was said to be moving complacently along, with head and shoulders only above the mud, because "he had a good mule under him," were among the facetiae retailed in the camps.

There were no sidewalks, except as they were extemporized from boxes of Virginia tobacco (then a drug in the market) or barrel staves; at each street corner were gathered crowds, awaiting their turn to pick their way across these stepping-blocks through the mud.

Such was the Winter of 1849. Hundreds were daily arriving, by sea and by land, filling the lodging-houses and adding to the number of dwellers in tents; in the interior the discomforts were still greater, and many, fearing that supplies would be cut off, by reason of impassable roads, made their way to the city. Premonitions of the cholera, which was then stalking across the country with the emigrants, were already apparent; exposure, and lack of proper food and comforts, and perhaps dissipation, added to the general sickness, and increased the number of deaths; many were found in the streets and vacant lots, or lying dead in the tents, and were buried by the city authorities. My old letters refer to the selfishness which generally prevailed, when in the general rush and scramble the sick were left to perish; perhaps I was not fitted to judge impartially of the causes for so much suffering and death, but it is certain that I saw a remarkable number of cases, and its effect upon me was very dispiriting; despite my naturally hopeful temperament, I frequently gave way to homesickness the most depressing.

On one memorable Sunday, I strolled out of the city to the summit of Russian Hill, on the apex of which were three graves of Russian sailors, buried, as the rude head boards showed, several years before, from vessels belonging to "Russian Possessions" on the Northwest Coast. The strong westerly winds were blowing a mournful requiem as it seemed to me. Home and friends never had seemed so far away; never was my sense of loneliness more complete, and I threw myself upon the ground and cried as though my heart would break.

With all the disposing causes towards dissipation created by such feelings, which I knew were experienced by thousands in those early days; with the attractions which the open saloons and gambling establishments presented (the only homes for hundreds); the almost entire absence of the society and influence of virtuous women, it is remarkable that so large a proportion of the younger men resisted the temptation toward evil habits. May not the prayers of good mothers, sisters, wives or sweethearts, have served as shields against the tempter?

As midwinter approached, and the reports from the mines more unsatisfactory, all thought of going there was abandoned, and the closing of our baking establishment made it necessary that I should turn my attention to some other means of livelihood; I had already a strong impulse towards independence of action—in other words, clerking or working for others was distasteful—so I preferred, if possible, an independent business where a small capital could be used. As I look upon the matter, from my present standpoint of experience, I incline toward the belief that it would have been better to have attached myself to some respectable and correct-dealing business house, until my habits of business had been formed and established.

The readiness to take up new enterprises became a habit, which remained with me for many years, and even now, when advancing years and greater responsibilities have made me more conservative, the impulse to look kindly toward new ventures and enterprises is very great, and has, at times, proved quite costly. This may be due, in large part, to a naturally hopeful temperament.

One of the business episodes at this time, was a brief contract to put together a number of ready-made zinc, or corrugated iron houses, imported from some Eastern city, packed and numbered, really requiring but little mechanical skill to erect, although my lack of knowledge of how to drive a nail without splitting the wood, furnished my partner in the enterprise with considerable amusement at my expense.

My visits to the restaurants and coffee-stands among the tents in Happy Valley and in other parts of the city, before referred to, convinced me that for the capital involved they were productive of large profits, and that the management of one of these enterprises was quite within the scope of my ability, so my next venture was in that direction; I had observed that the largest number of the new arrivals landed on or about Clark's Point, and followed a trail which led over the edge of the hill, or along the beach, struck Jackson Street about where a small street, called Balance Street, now enters it, and thence made their way to the Post Office, on Clay Street; the waters of the bay, at this point, reached west of Sansome Street. It seemed to me, that a stand at this place would attract a good deal of custom from the newly-arrived, whom I knew, from experience, would have keen appetites for the good things usually displayed in such establishments.

I promptly leased a piece of ground of suitable dimensions, adjoining the easterly side-wall of the old Excelsior Restaurant building, which served as one side of the establishment, which I constructed of canvas.

It was rather a pretentious affair, with neatly-scalloped edges to the awning, or roof, and a counter front, at which the customer stood while taking his lunch.

A highly-colored lithograph of the City Hall and Park in New York, handsomely framed, had the place of honor on the wall, and served to denote the locality where the proprietor (in the vernacular) "hailed" from.

This also served to suggest a name, and the "City Hall Lunch" (painted by me) in letters on the front of the counter, invited the passers by, not less than the glistening black tin "hot coffee" urn, the toothsome doughnuts, pies and cookies.

This enterprise proved a success from the beginning, and I thoroughly enjoyed it. I had not been long under weigh, when, among the new arrivals who came to my counter one day, appeared an old New York acquaintance, Henry I. Beers, a year or two older than myself; frequent intercourse, and a regard growing from home associations, induced me to tender him an interest in the enterprise; this was accepted, and we enlarged, to some extent, our operations. Our success brought us an offer for our establishment from a Mr.——, an elderly gentleman, who at one time had been an extensive ship-owner in New York. A price ($500) was at length agreed upon, and at the close of the week (May 4th, 1850) we were to pass over the "City Hall Lunch" to its new proprietor; very early that morning I was aroused by the cry of fire, and going out found an extensive conflagration raging in the center of the city. From the experience of the previous December, I knew that its course would only be stayed by the bay, toward which it was traveling; with a view to making the most of the remaining opportunities, and knowing that, if it extended and took Jackson Street, all the restaurants would be destroyed, I returned to my place of business, having secured an extra supply of materials for sale. I was not disappointed; the fire engines were stationed on the beach near by, to take water from the bay, and hungry firemen were frequent patrons, my supplies being exhausted before noon.

The gains of the day were very handsome, and these were tendered to Mr.——, to release us from the contract to sell, but he declined, paid us the stipulated price in gold dust, and Saturday night closed our proprietorship.

I ought to say here, that the buildings which were erected in the neighborhood, soon shut out the site of the "City Hall Lunch" from the advantages which the trail from Clark's Point gave it, and the business soon ceased to be profitable. The location is at present occupied by the Genesee Mills, on Gold Street.

In March of this year I visited Sacramento for the first time, by invitation of a relative, Mr. Waterbury, who was part owner and Captain of the schooner *Alfred*. I accompanied him on a voyage up the river, for the purpose of painting the name on the stern and otherwise decorating her. The vessel was loaded with ready-made houses, made in Boston, and consigned to John Q. Packard, the principal proprietor of one of the towns then coming into existence at the mouth of Feather River, where it empties into the Sacramento: Marysville and Yuba City, of equal pretensions, and like most of the numerous paper towns of that period, equally promising. I think Packard's town, of which our houses were to form a part, was Yuba City. Whether because of more material advantages, or greater enterprise, Marysville speedily outstripped it.

We took on board a number of passengers, among whom was a slightly-built, studious lad of seventeen, fond of reading Byron, who was going to Yuba City as clerk for Pollard. This lad, after a career of vicissitudes, and rather a fast life in Marysville, became an active politician—candidate of the Republican Party for Governor of California, and for many years filled the responsible position of Secretary of the United States Senate.

Our trip was a slow and tedious one, and we were nearly a week reaching Sacramento, where we hauled up alongside the bank, for the levee at that time had not been constructed; the flood of the previous January had in part subsided, but the water yet stood in all the lower places and depressions; the effects were seen in every direction, many of the houses had been washed from their slight foundations or thrown askew, while a line of mud or slime, marked on the side-walls of the buildings about eight feet from the ground, showed that to have been the depth of the overflow.

After visiting Sutter Fort, of historic interest, which then retained the walls and enclosed buildings which gave it character, and laying in some fresh meats and other supplies, we took in our cable tow, and endeavored to make our way, by our own efforts, towards our destination; this was quite as tedious, the most of the way being made by hauling, the line being attached to trees on the bank on either side.

We made our way until within a few miles of Hock Farm, the home of Captain Sutter, when, for some reason, our schooner was tied to the bank, the houses were put ashore, and we waited for a favorable wind to return us to the bay.

Passengers and sailors left us and started afoot for the mines, leaving Captain Waterbury, his mate, the cook and myself to work the schooner. After several days delay, we cast off, and with the chain cable over the bow as a drag, to steady the vessel and serve as a rudder, we backed down, until with more favorable wind and more sailing room we could utilize our sails.

On the return voyage, I experienced the infliction which all old Californians will remember so well, which no amount of personal cleanliness could avoid for those who traveled at all, and were obliged to occupy the so-called hotels of those days; the way-side places fairly swarmed with disgusting vermin, which were carried about from place to place in the blankets and clothes of travelers. The berths of our schooner were alive with them, but this I only discovered when the peculiar irritation excited my suspicion and produced an investigation; there was then no help for it, but I was the first to get ashore when we again dropped anchor off San Francisco, and I hastened to purchase a new outfit and buried the infected garments out of sight. Even now, I experience a peculiar crawling sensation when my memory reverts to the sickening effect, the self-degradation I felt when I made the discovery.

Our next movement established Beers and myself as proprietors of a tidy restaurant on Jackson Street, near Montgomery Street. With questionable wisdom we had taken a few months lease, and erected a building; I had also built one adjoining, in connection with a shipmate named Booth, to rent. The landlord would not renew our lease at expiration, so in July of that year (1850) Beers and I were installed in the "New World Restaurant," a one-story and a half building, which we erected on ground of which we had a lease, near the head of Cunningham's Wharf, then the landing place of the *New World* and other Sacramento steamers. Here we added to our business small groceries —"miners' supplies"—and did a neat business fitting out parties for the mines.

The sensation of the hour, during our occupancy of this place, was the arrival of refugees from Sacramento fleeing before the cholera, which was decimating that city. This dread disease had stalked by the side of the emigrants across the Plains, marking its path by new-made graves at every step; it accompanied those who came by the way of the Isthmus of Darien and Nicaragua, and daily burials at sea, from the over-crowded and poorly provisioned steamers, marked its presence on shipboard.

The condition of the newly-arrived emigrants, especially in the warm and humid atmosphere of Sacramento, rendered them peculiarly susceptible to the attacks of the cholera, and the mortality was in frightful proportion to the population.

There were a large number of cases in San Francisco, but its ravages were light compared with the other cities. By especial attention to our diet, and prompt use of such remedies as were used in those days, when the system indicated disturbance, we passed through safely, although my partner, being of large and fleshy habit, and fond of the table, was thoroughly frightened, on at least one occasion. In the excess of my zeal, on the first alarm, I administered the castor oil and laudanum so liberally to him, that poor Beers thought the remedy quite equal, in its effects, to the disease.

Early in the Winter of 1850 we appear to have gone back to Jackson Street, having abandoned the restaurant business and put out our sign as General Merchants.

The card before me reads:

*DORNIN & BEERS,*
*WHOLESALE AND RETAIL GROCERS*
*AND PROVISION DEALERS,*
*16 JACKSON STREET, NORTH SIDE,*
*—BETWEEN MONTGOMERY AND*
*SANSOME STREETS.*

*GOODS SOLD ON COMMISSION.*
*GEO. D. DORNIN     H. IRVING BEERS.*

So far as we could see, this venture was in the right direction; we were young (both under age) full of hope, with spirits buoyant, and popular among our fellow merchants; our stand was a good one; my partner was a calculating, money-making man, and we were steadily accumulating stock and adding to our capital. Among the episodes during this period, was the Gold Bluff excitement, which carried hundreds on a wild chase to the mines, which were said to exist on the bluff and beach near Trinidad Bay, the beach sands which when uncovered by the washing of the sea were rich in gold, and numerous expeditions were fitted out to work them. With a view to avail ourselves on the opportunity for trade, Beers and I put up an outfit of supplies and sent them, with Beers in charge, on the propeller *Eudora*, to establish a trading establishment near the mines. Through stress of weather, the deck-load was thrown overboard, the ship put about and returned to port, and thus ended our venture. With the opening of Spring came overtures from

Captain——, of the *Eudora*, to join our firm as a silent partner; appreciating the advantages of additional cash capital, we commenced "taking stock," for the purpose of determining the amount necessary to be put in by the Captain as its equivalent; this we had concluded on Saturday, the 4th day of May, 1851. On the evening of that day my partner had gone to the theatre, while I remained at the store, busy with the books and putting the figures together; from these I determined that the actual net worth of the firm was about $10,000. I retired to my bed, in the upper story of our store building, late in the evening, and for some time laid awake indulging in pleasant and satisfactory musings over the flattering prospects before me. I should be twenty-one the following Winter, and, fully determined to carry out the original plan of going home when I was of age, I should either sell my interest in the business, or so arrange with my partner that I should go, to return again, for the future already gave indications that California would be something more than a temporary abiding place. No cloud dimmed the picture, and with these happy thoughts uppermost I dropped asleep.

About half-past eleven I was awakened by the dreaded clang of the fire bell. Going out, I found a fire raging on Clay Street, opposite the Plaza; soon it crossed Kearney, gathering force as it went; making my way to Tucker's, who then (with a partner named Reeve) kept a fine stock of jewelry on Commercial Street, I waited until the threatening flames began to work toward the rear of his store, and then assisted him and others to carry his stock to a supposed place of safety, a brick building on Montgomery Street; thence I went to my friend Newell's, whose new paper, the "Pacific Star," was to be issued for the first time on the following Monday. While tugging at his heavy cases of type, I noticed that the wind had changed, and the flames were rolling in huge volumes in the direction of my own store, and that no time was to be lost if I expected to save anything.

Hastening there, I found my cousin, Captain John B. Dornin (who had arrived a few weeks previously in command of the bark *"Oscar"*), he had brought his crew with him, and all were waiting to "lend a hand." Opening the doors, we all set to with a will, but as the flames traveled fast, the goods saved were again moved, and finally became so mixed with the mass of similar goods piled along the slope of Telegraph Hill, that identification became impossible.

Worn out with the exertions of the night, I threw myself down on a pile of merchandise and soon fell into a deep sleep, from which I awoke, blackened, with head and eyebrows singed, about ten o'clock on a beautiful Sabbath morning. The fire, which had swept everything from the place of its origin to the bay, was spending its force in the vicinity of Clark's Point; below me lay the ashes of the city; here and there a brick wall marked the remains of the few brick buildings, not one of which stood the test of fire.

All that remained of my own neat "fortune" of the day before, was the few dray-loads of merchandise on which I had been lying. After a refreshing cup of coffee, given me by the good lady near whose house I had been sleeping, I made my way to the site of our store. I had taken care to save our books, and from these I found that our indebtedness was slight; on my proposition, my partner agreed to pay this, take the remainder of the stock saved, and pay me $100, and with this sum I started [out into] the world again. My next venture is indicated by the advertisement cut from the "Alta California," which my scrap book develops. It reads thus:

> *GEORGE D. DORNIN, (formerly of Dornin & Beers,) will attend to plain Painting, Lining, and any other kind of business. Residence at Tucker's Restaurant, on the Plaza. Slates for Orders at Otten & Cohn's, Gold St., "Point Market," Pacific Wharf, and at W. O. Wilson & Co.'s Grocery, Pacific St., two doors above the Hospital.* —*May 23, 1851.*

My friend Tucker's splendid stock of jewelry, which, with so much labor we had removed to a supposed "fireproof" [box], was consumed with the rest, but with characteristic energy, he had rented a new building on the Clay Street side of the Plaza, and established a restaurant, where, at meal times, I assisted him at the tables, thus saving the cost of board and lodgings—no inconsiderable item. During this time I was witness of one of those extraordinary movements for which the early history of San Francisco was noted; the first execution by the Vigilance Committee of 1851.

Mr. Tucker and I had been strolling down town in the evening, when we heard rumors that a man had been arrested for some crime by a Vigilance Committee, who were then in session trying him; we made our way to their rooms on Battery near Pine Street, and joined the crowd who were discussing the matter outside.

Toward midnight, Mr. Samuel Brannan came out, and, mounting a sand-bank opposite, addressed the crowd; he said that a "Sidney cove," named Jenkins, had been arrested while making off with a small safe, which he had stolen; that he had been convicted and sentenced to be hung, and he (Brannan) asked if the people approved of the verdict; the crowd (as crowds always do) shouted "aye." We waited about an hour or more, until, believing that the execution would be postponed for some reason, we strolled towards home.

We were in the neighborhood of the corner of Clay and Kearney Streets, when hearing noises behind us, we looked and beheld approaching through Clay Street, an irregular procession of men, with pistols drawn, marching with the prisoner in their midst; approaching the flagstaff which then graced the center of the unfenced and unimproved "Plaza," some of those who were in the advance, were about to use the halyards for the "hangman's rope" when shouts were raised, "Don't disgrace the liberty pole!" and the prisoner was carried forward across the

Plaza to the old adobe building, formerly the Custom House, which stood on the north-west corner of the square; a beam across the deep-projecting cornice on the south end of the old adobe was improvised as a gallows, over this a rope was hastily thrown, a noose was made and placed around the doomed man's neck, many willing hands seized the rope, and, at a signal, Jenkins was run up, his head striking the beam with a thud.

Excited as I was, I was not yet prepared to enjoy such scenes, and I would gladly have gotten away, but I was pressed by the crowd, so that I was obliged to be a spectator, and, until the crowd began to disperse I was kept standing within a short distance of the hanged man. By this time it was two o'clock in the morning, when, excited and nervous over the scenes which I had witnessed, I sought my room, which, it will be remembered, was in Tucker's Restaurant, on the south side of the Plaza; when I awoke in the morning, the body of Jenkins was still hanging, dangling in the air.

The executioners apparently had disappeared; here and there, a group of people stood discussing the events of the night, and speculating concerning the results.

Later in the morning, the Coroner took charge of the body, summoned a jury and took such testimony as was available. The jury returned a verdict, implicating by name several of the most prominent of the participants.

This was promptly followed by a card in all the papers, signed by a large number of citizens representing all interests in the city, claiming to be equal participants with those who were singled out by the Coroner's Jury. The organization also published a statement of the causes of their action, and of its future intentions, of which the following is the preamble:

*"It has become apparent to the citizens of San Francisco that there is*

*no security to life and property, either under the regulation of society as it at present exists, or under the laws as now administered, therefore, the citizens whose names are hereunto attached, do unite themselves into an association, for the maintenance of the peace and good order of society and the preservation of the lives and property of the citizens of San Francisco, and do bind ourselves, each unto the other, to do and perform every lawful act for the maintenance of law and order, and to sustain the laws when faithfully and properly administered. But we are determined that no thief, burglar, incendiary or assassin shall escape punishment, either by the quibbles of the law, the insecurity of prisons, the carelessness or corruption of the police, or laxity of those who pretend to administer justice."*

This was the formation of the Vigilance Committee of 1851; though not an active member of the organization, I was thoroughly in sympathy with its motives, and, if I had been older, should undoubtedly have been an active participant.

The Committee maintained its organization during the entire Summer; they made many arrests, in each case giving those arrested fair and impartial trials; some were banished from the State, others against whom the evidence was not conclusive, were discharged; three others, besides Jenkins, were executed. One, named Stuart, who was the self-confessed leader of the gang of desperadoes who had so outraged the community, was hung from a derrick at the foot of Market Street, and two others, Whitaker and McKenzie, were hung from the windows of the rooms of the Vigilance Committee, on Battery Street.

Efforts were made by the regularly constituted authorities to suppress the Vigilance Committee, but the majority of the people of San Francisco were so pronounced in its favor, that their efforts were unavailing, and the Committee, during the term of its active existence, actually superceded the judicial and municipal authorities, and possessed the city.

It was subsequently disbanded, subject to the call of its Executive Committee. Such was the effect of the good work of the organization, that not until the Summer of 1856 was it found necessary to call together the forces; at that time I was living in the interior, and did not see its practical workings.

It is a matter of history, however, that the Vigilance Committee of 1856 held possession of the city, and executed its mandates for several months; its headquarters on Sacramento Street, east of Front Street, were barricaded with bags filled with sand, whence its name, "Fort Gunny Bags"; four men were hung by its orders, for the crime of murder, and one committed suicide while under arrest and in its cells. When the Committee laid down its authority, it exhibited its military power by parading a well organized and equipped army of 6,000 men.

From it sprang the "Peoples' Party," which, for several years, elected the municipal officers, and under which San Francisco became the best governed city in the United States.

Keeping a restaurant proved too slow a method of making money for one of Mr. Tucker's ambitious temperament, and during June he made preparations to re-establish himself in his old business as a jeweler; my own time had been pretty well employed at sign painting, lining and paper-hanging, a portion of the time in the employ of Frank Baker, upholsterer, at $10 per day. When the new movement was decided upon, Tucker offered me a percentage of the profits, in lieu of salary, which I accepted. A store was secured on the west side of Montgomery Street, the second north of Sacramento Street, which we opened in the latter part of June, 1851.

The business had many vicissitudes, chiefly through lack of ready capital to command a large stock at the best prices. It thus happened that during the following Spring the discussions of the question of ways and means were frequent, and these resulted in an expedition to the mines, with a view to working off some of the more unsaleable stock and raising a considerable sum of ready money.

The disposition of merchandize by lottery (or raffle, as the method was designated) was of common occurrence, and met the speculative humor of the times; in council with our friends, it was determined that I should be sent into the interior for this purpose, and by advice of Mr. Samuel Langton, the Pioneer Expressman of Nevada and Sierra Counties, Nevada City was decided upon as the objective point of the trip. A good catalogue was made up of five hundred articles, aggregating in value, at "catalogue prices," $10,000; tickets and sensational advertising matter were arranged, and in May I started for the mines.

This movement formed one of the pivotal points in my life's history. Anticipating a speedy return and that my stay would, at any rate, be but temporary, I remained fifteen years a resident of Nevada County, was married, and had all of my children (save one) born to me there, and was twice elected its representative in the State Legislature.

The journey to Nevada City was made by boat to Sacramento, thence by stage. I had as a traveling companion an old printer named Russell, full of wise philosophy, as became his craft, and liberal in his counsel and advice to his young friend.

I remember that he was especially profound in his political opinions; the campaign of 1852 was then active, the great agitation over the slavery question, which culminated in the civil war nine years later, excited the country; the old Whig party was making its final struggle, with Gen'l Winfield Scott as its standard bearer for President, and for him, the following November, I cast my maiden vote. I was young and ardent, a hater of oppression in any form, and naturally gravitated towards free soil doctrines; I was pronounced in my opinions, and perhaps needed the caution of my older and more experienced friend, that, as I was going into a locality where men of extreme pro-slavery views were numerous and influential, and where, as a rule, in politics Northern men had "no rights which the Southerner was bound to respect," it was the part of worldly wisdom to be reticent.

We reached our destination in due season, where I secured a room for displaying my wares, in the principal hotel, then known as the Gregory House; distributed my posters and catalogues throughout the town, and then proceeded to establish agencies for the sale of tickets in the neighboring mining camps. As there were very few graded roads, crossing the steep canons of the Yubas and their branches, the journeys were necessarily made on horseback, which with the freedom and novelty of my position, I enjoyed thoroughly. I was always made welcome by the miners in their camps, and to this day I retain the most pleasant recollections of my trips to Red Dog, Little York, Steep Hollow, French Corral, You Bet, etc., for such was the peculiar nomenclature in those days. The goods which I had taken into Nevada made a fine display, and as the element of chance, which attended their distribution, is always attractive, my enterprise became very popular, and the tickets met with rapid sales, all classes of the community holding them, in the hope of securing for a small consideration some of the more valuable articles.

In those days, games of chance had not encountered the ban of public opinion, to that extent which, with more settled society, prevails in these later days; gambling was carried on in the mining towns with open doors. It is proper to say, however, that the Legislature had made some feeble efforts to correct the evil, and among other statutes had enacted one prohibiting lotteries; of the effect of this, upon my subsequent enterprise, I will speak hereafter.

I had set the day for the drawing and distribution, having fully decided to revisit Nevada [City], with another outfit for my individual account, with the profits of which I hoped to carry out my cherished desire to return home.

A committee of leading citizens was appointed, to whom I turned over the management of the distribution; they selected a young girl, who, blindfolded, was to draw the winning numbers from the large wheel, which was placed in a large window in the second story of the Gregory House, in full view of the crowd, which filled the street in front.

All went off, with apparent satisfaction, and the result netted a handsome profit on the cost of the goods to Mr. Tucker. I left immediately for San Francisco, settled with him, and then arranged to take my due from him in merchandise, and, with a sufficient stock in addition to make an effective catalogue, I again visited Nevada [City] and established my agencies for the sale of tickets for the second "Raffle."

I reckoned without my host, in concluding that there was no dissatisfaction with the first, as it transpired; when my second was well advanced, the Grand Jury, then in session, had the matter brought to their attention, and, finding the statute against lotteries could be made to reach over and cover my "Raffle," found two indictments for violation of the statute. I promptly called on my friend, the County Judge, and after consultation with him and other legal friends, I left the matter in the hands of Judge Buckner, a lawyer of prominence.

I had the fullest sympathy of the community, particularly of the ladies, and the approval of my own conscience that, notwithstanding the allotments of the wares was left to chance, there was no one wronged, and in every respect the entire transaction was perfectly honest and fair.

I was particularly anxious that there should be no delay or embarrassment; all I had was involved in it, and upon its success depended not only the payment for that portion due Mr. Tucker, but to get my own from it.

It was, furthermore, my last venture to accumulate enough to return "home," the three years which I had fixed as the limit of absence having about elapsed.

It was therefore arranged by my friends, that it was most expedient to plead guilty to one indictment, and enter a *nolle prosequi* for the other; the Judge should then impose the minimum fine, which I should pay, and could go on with my enterprise. All this was done, and in due season the distribution took place; but the effect of the prosecution had been mischievous, and misunderstandings created, which affected materially the sale of tickets; the result was a loss on the original investment.

After settling with Mr. Tucker, I determined to return to Nevada [City] and make it my home; I had formed many pleasant associations, and there was a freedom and elasticity in the mountain life, which was very fascinating to my young mind. Moreover, I had not gotten over the disposition to make new ventures. Among the propositions for the future, which seemed most promising, was the establishment of a dry goods business, and to this I was induced by the representations of my lady friends of Nevada [City], that an American establishment would meet with general patronage, and would necessarily be successful; my next venture was in that direction, having formed a copartnership with George O. Kilbourne, a young man from Vermont, who was pursuing the business of daguerreotyping; we hired and fitted up a two story building, the lower story for dry goods and the upper for the business of taking daguerreotypes. The Winter of 1852 was a very severe one; snow fell to a great depth, and by reason of impassable roads leading from the lower country, supplies of all kinds reached a very high figure—flour, at one time, reaching one dollar per pound in some portions of the mines.

In Down[i]eville, such was the scarcity, that public meetings were held, at which it was decided that all able-bodied men, without family incumbrances, should make their way out to the settlements below, so that the supplies in town would be sufficient to maintain those who were compelled to remain.

Nevada [City] received many of these, who came foot sore, snow-

GEORGE D. DORNIN'S GRASS VALLEY STUDIO.

blinded, and blanket-laden from the mines above us.

At Grass Valley, it was said, a team loaded with supplies for a merchant in Nevada [City] was stopped by the citizens, and the teamster compelled to sell the flour, potatoes, etc., of which his load was composed. Flour at that time commanded fifty cents per pound, and other necessaries in proportion.

Notwithstanding this condition of affairs, the Winter was not without its enjoyments. Kilbourne and I kept "Bachelor's Hall," having our own kitchen and being our own cooks, in a room attached to the store; the snow furnished excellent sleighing, and we extemporized sleighs from dry goods boxes and crockery crates; we entered heartily into the social amusements of the season. By the Spring of 1853 I had begun to realize that success in merchandizing requires especial training and adaptability, and that our competitors, by reason of these qualifications, and larger capital, were underselling us, and taking the trade of the very ladies who had protested loudest against the Jewish merchants, and induced us to enter the lists.

With the same readiness to drop an enterprise which I found distasteful, I determined to get out of the dry goods department of our business; giving close attention to the manipulation of the daguerreotype process, I became proficient in the art, and in the early Summer of 1853, disposed of my interest in the firm and removed to Grass Valley, a very flourishing town five miles distant, supported by extensive quartz and placer mines. There I put out my sign as daguerreotypist. Again the sky was full of promise; the business was lucrative, and my sanguine temperament induced me to purchase a lot and building on the main street, for which I employed an architect and carpenter to refit and furnish for my purposes.

In October of this year (1853) I was married to Miss Sarah A. Baldwin, who had arrived about a year previously with her parents, from Medford, Massachusetts.

With this "new departure" and a brief retrospect of the events which shaped my subsequent course, these reminiscences will be brought to a close. I have not attempted to write history—better pens than my own have given the world the annals of California and the history of the settlement of the early days, and my children will seek information in them, should these stories of their father's life prompt them to further inquiry.

Our first child was born to us in December, 1854; in September of the following year, the great fire which destroyed the entire town of Grass Valley, burned my building and its contents; the dwelling house of my wife's mother, with whom we were boarding, a portion of which we had fitted up, all was destroyed, except one trunk of apparatus and a few articles of household goods.

As soon as the ashes were cold, I contracted for and commenced rebuilding on my business lot, but the effects of the fire were very depressing upon all similar branches of business; a few months spent with a blue tent among the mining camps, as a traveling "artist," while it pleased my nomadic tastes, had lost its old-time fascinations, as my changed social condition made family and fireside more attractive.

With the close of the year, I determined to try my fortunes elsewhere; among the camps which I had visited, the new one then coming into notoriety, known as San Juan, situated on the ridge dividing the South and Middle Yubas, held out the greatest promise. I arranged with the party who held my mortgage upon my lot to pay off the incumbrances in consideration of a deed to the property, and on New Year's morning, 1856, took my departure to the new field of operations. I hired a

DORNIN'S
SKY-LIGHT GALLERY,
In his New Building
KNICKERBOCKER HALL, MAIN STREET,
Opposite Beatty House, Grass Valley.
☞ Daguerreotypes taken in Superior Styles.

wagon in Nevada [City] to take me and my trunk of daguerreotype apparatus to my destination; after paying the hire and tolls, I found myself the possessor of one dollar and fifty cents, with which to commence the world anew. I was met with warm hearts and open hands at San Juan (North), where so many pleasant years were subsequently spent.

Theodore Green, who then kept the store, corner of Main and Flume Streets, gave me permission to put out my sign and use his store as a display room, and subsequently, when I brought my wife and child over, the small rooms in the rear formed our abiding place, until our own house was ready for occupancy. Green and Sears (Wm. H.) were then fitting up the Sierra Nevada Hotel, and my application to them for the "job" of papering it was readily granted, so that, between hanging wall paper, taking daguerreotypes and painting signs, my time was fully occupied, and I soon acquired enough to purchase a lot for a home and operating room; ordered lumber for a house, then went to Grass Valley, and on the 14th of February, 1856, with wife and baby on a wagon loaded with our little stock of household goods, "emigrated" to San Juan, where we remained for eleven years.

With economy we built up our home, and I gradually accumulated business around me; the strain was heavy at times; under Lincoln's administration, I was appointed Postmaster, and in addition held the position of express agent, telegraph operator, insurance agent, owned and operated two stage lines connecting the towns above and below us on "the Ridge," kept the books of the Middle Yuba Canal and Water Company, and added a small newspaper, magazine, and tree business, in its season. I was always an active partisan, and threw myself heartily into the movement for the formation of the Republican Party; if my instincts had not then tended that way, the influence of such men as Benjamin P. Avery, R. H. Farquhar, Theodore Green, and similar choice spirits, who formed the excellent society of North San Juan in those days, would have directed me.

We had formed one of the first Republican Clubs during the Fremont campaign of 1856—the Rocky Mountain Club—there were seventeen of us, originally, to withstand the jeers, and to be hailed as "Black Republicans," Negro Worshipers," etc., in the party slang of the day.

In 1865 I was given the nomination for the Legislature by the Republican County Convention; the county being strongly Union or Republican, the nomination was equivalent to an election, but there was a schism in the Republican ranks, growing out of the opposition to the leadership of the Hon. A. A. Sargent; this opposition organized a "bolt" from the regular nominations, and put a new ticket in the field, expecting to draw sufficiently from Democratic affiliations to overcome the regular Republican majority, or at least so cripple Mr. Sargent in his own county as to destroy his prestige for further honors. The result of the election in September, was the success of the entire Republican ticket by handsome majorities. My majority in my own township and precinct, gratified me exceedingly, leading my associates on the ticket largely.

The event of the session of the Legislature of 1865-6, which I recall with the greatest satisfaction, is the privilege which was given me to record my vote in the affirmative, on the resolution to ratify the proposed amendment to the Constitution of the United States abolishing slavery.

With the opening of 1867, came propositions from the manager of a prominent Eastern Insurance company (the Phoenix of Hartford, whose local agency I had held since 1863) to accept the position as special field agent; to this profession I had given a good deal of attention, and in the previous October (1866) I had made an overland trip to Oregon, to present a memorial on insurance matters to the Legislature of that State, then in session at Salem; these negotiations resulted in my appointment as special agent and adjuster for a term of years, and an opportunity to visit, in that capacity, all portions of California, Oregon

NORTH SAN JUAN. HALF-PLATE DAGUERREOTYPE BY CHARLES D. DORNIN.

and Nevada, an opportunity which I greatly coveted and enjoyed, and which was of great advantage to my physical health.

The approaching political campaign, brought with it desires from our party leaders in Nevada County, to return me as candidate for re-election to the Legislature: this resulted in my renomination, and, although the party was not successful in the State at large, the county ticket was elected by fair majorities. Subsequent to the election in September, I broke up my home in North San Juan, and removed my family to San Jose, the declining interests of the former place, and the growing needs of my family for better educational opportunities, as well as the new business arrangements, making this course advisable.

With the usual routine of Legislative duties, and especial attention on my part, to the important insurance legislation, which was among the most exciting of the measures before that body, the session of 1867-8 passed. At its close, I gladly retired from the cares and responsibilities of public life, entirely satisfied thereafter to attend to my private business. To the profession of under-writing I have since been attached, and in all human probability it will be my vocation for life. After four years of service with the company first mentioned, I received the appointment, in the Spring of 1871, of General Agent for the Fireman's Fund Insurance Company, in which capacity, in company with Mr. D. J. Staples, its President, I visited Chicago and New York, to adjust the heavy losses of the Company in the great fire in the former city.

I was subsequently made Vice-President, and in 1873 elected Secretary, which position I now hold.

As I close these reminiscences, I write in a pleasant home, built by us in 1874, in Berkeley, overlooking the Bay and City of San Francisco, and out through the Golden Gate, through whose portals our good ship entered "*thirty years ago.*"

Five children surround our table: George William, born December 19, 1854; Mary Avis, born September 11, 1861; John Cushing, born July 10, 1865; Julia, born July 29, 1867; and Alice, born August 2, 1870.

The marriage of George, in July, 1879, to Miss Hattie H. Ball, adds a sixth child to our fold.

Our little Avis, born May, 1859, lies in the village churchyard in North San Juan, where we laid her to rest, one stormy day in March, 1861.

With gratitude to the Giver of all good for the many blessings we enjoy; for the often advantages which have followed seeming disasters; and the silver lining which has often illumined the darker clouds of my life, I give this record to my children.

Berkeley, California,
November, 1879.

*This edition of* THIRTY YEARS AGO
*is set in Bembo and Copperplate types.*
*The design and type composition are by Richard D. Moore*
*of Sacramento, California.*
*1,000 copies have been printed on archival paper*
*by Thomson-Shore of Dexter, Michigan, in August, 1995.*